Keywords:
Abstract Word Designs

are simply colorful designs
with form as function,
but they are also
one line poems/concepts
and you can word search if you like.

They are comprised of one background color each
and then only the "keywords" associated with it
(except for "spirit" which has a background photo
of ancient pictographs).

They are at once literal but figurative,
figurative but abstract.

They are:
i, spirit, imagination, nature, wanderlust, music, mystic,
esp, metaphor, demons, schism, artist, humor, party,
beer, baseball, usa, fff, science, spring, summer,
fall, winter, air, earth, water, fire,
simplicity, holy, love

Keywords:

i...

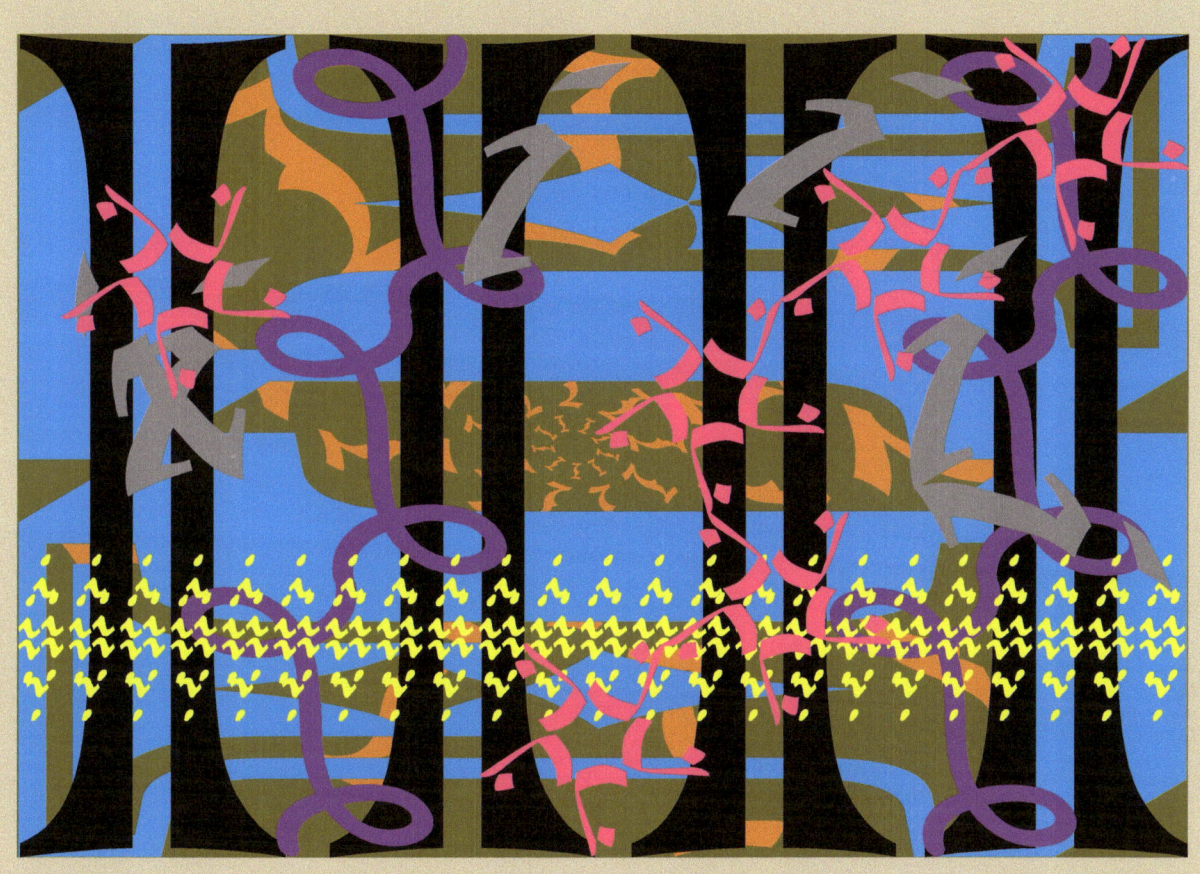

Keywords:

spirit, consciousness, intuition, belief, the reason, body, creation

Keywords:

imagination, illusion, fantasy, dream, chimera, aspiration, apparition, vision

Keywords:

nature, animals, humans, flora, fauna, land, water, sky

Keywords:

wanderlust, traveler, restless, explorer, discover, lost, journey

Keywords:

music, classical, electronic, folk, country, reggae, jazz, blues, rock n roll

Keywords:

mystic, poet, sage, shaman, wise guy

Keywords:

esp, hypnosis, clairvoyance, psychic, paranormal, yet another realm

Keywords:

metaphor, myth, symbolism, allegory, allusion, illusion, hidden meaning, om

Keywords:

demons, ghouls, vampires, zombies, werewolves, ghosts, monsters

.

Keywords:

schism, nationalism, racism, fanaticism, fundamentalism

Keywords:

artist, perform, comedy, drama, music, painting, writing, sensitivity, creativity

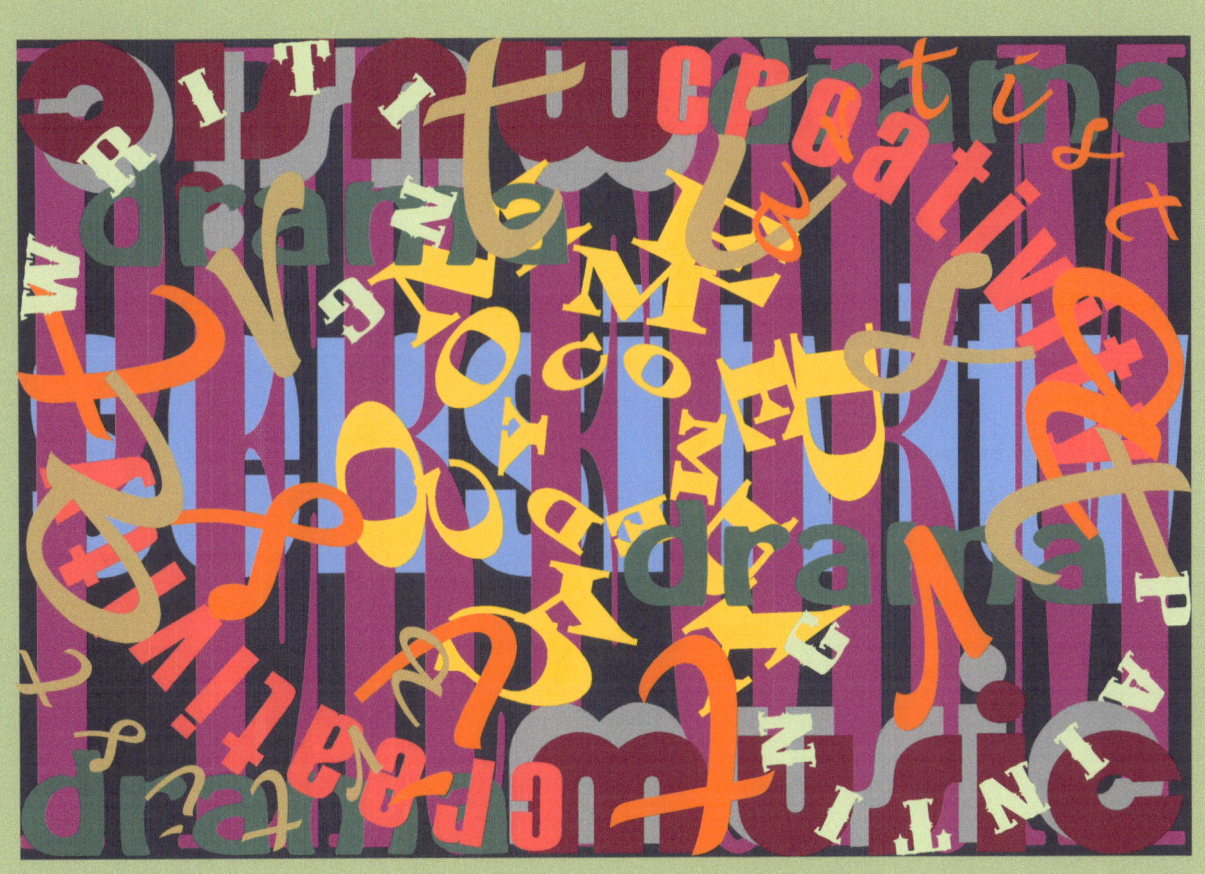

Keywords:

humor, comedy, wit, irony, parodies, satire, sarcasm

Keywords:

party, conversation, friendship, camaraderie, delicious, food, drink, laughter, flirt, kiss

Keywords:

beer, craft, malt, hops, nose, flavor, foam, buzz

Keywords:

baseball, bat, glove, ball, strike out, double play, rbi, home run, grand slam

Keywords:

usa, country, freedom, idealism, innovation, greed, righteousness, self, corporation, pomposity, compassion

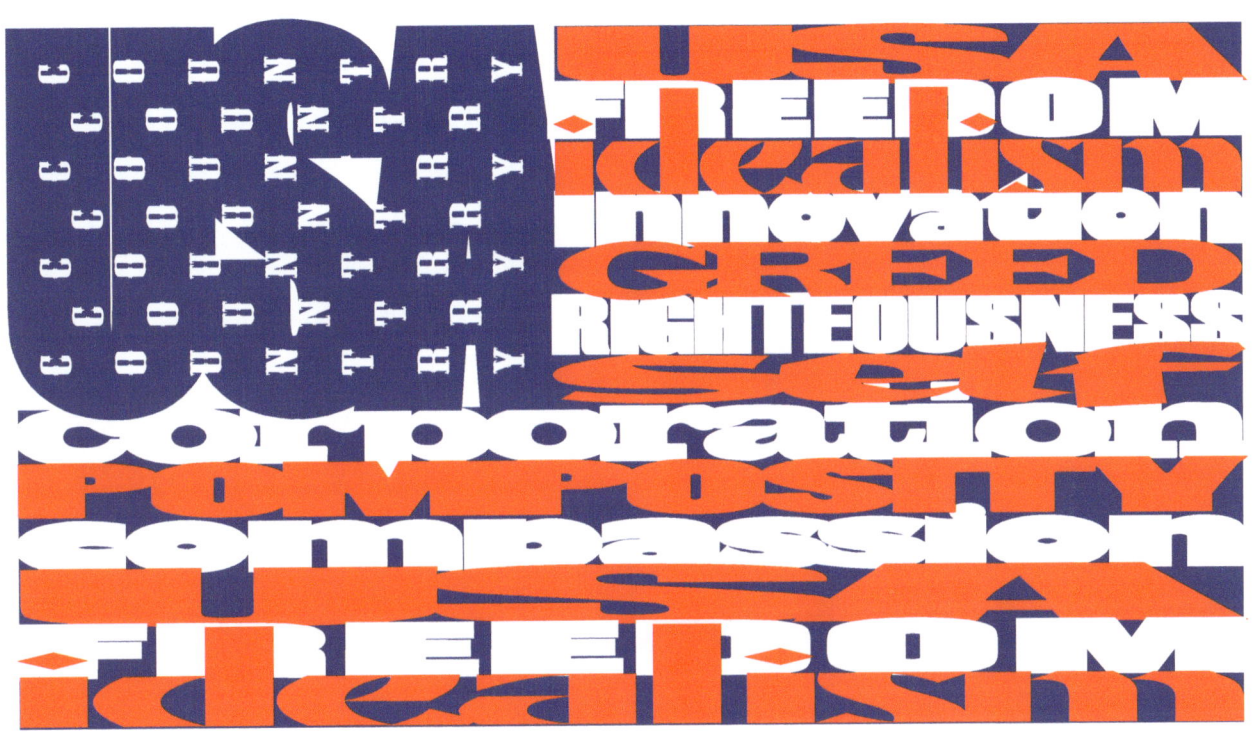

Keywords:

fff…

Keywords:

science, cut, solve, find, observe, objective, faith, skeptical, curiousity

Keywords:

spring, creeping, green, warm, rain

Keywords:

summer, thick, hot, blowing, sun

Keywords:

fall, dry, leaves, cool, moon

Keywords:

winter, cold, blue, glowing, night

Keywords:

air, breathe, fly, vent, storm, reveal, open, song

Keywords:

earth, rock, solid, sure, growth, dig, hold, home

Keywords:

water, ocean, cleanse, quench, drown, swim, fountain, life

Keywords:

fire, burn, purge, cook, hot, zeal, dance, warmth

Keywords:

simplicity, minimalism, stark

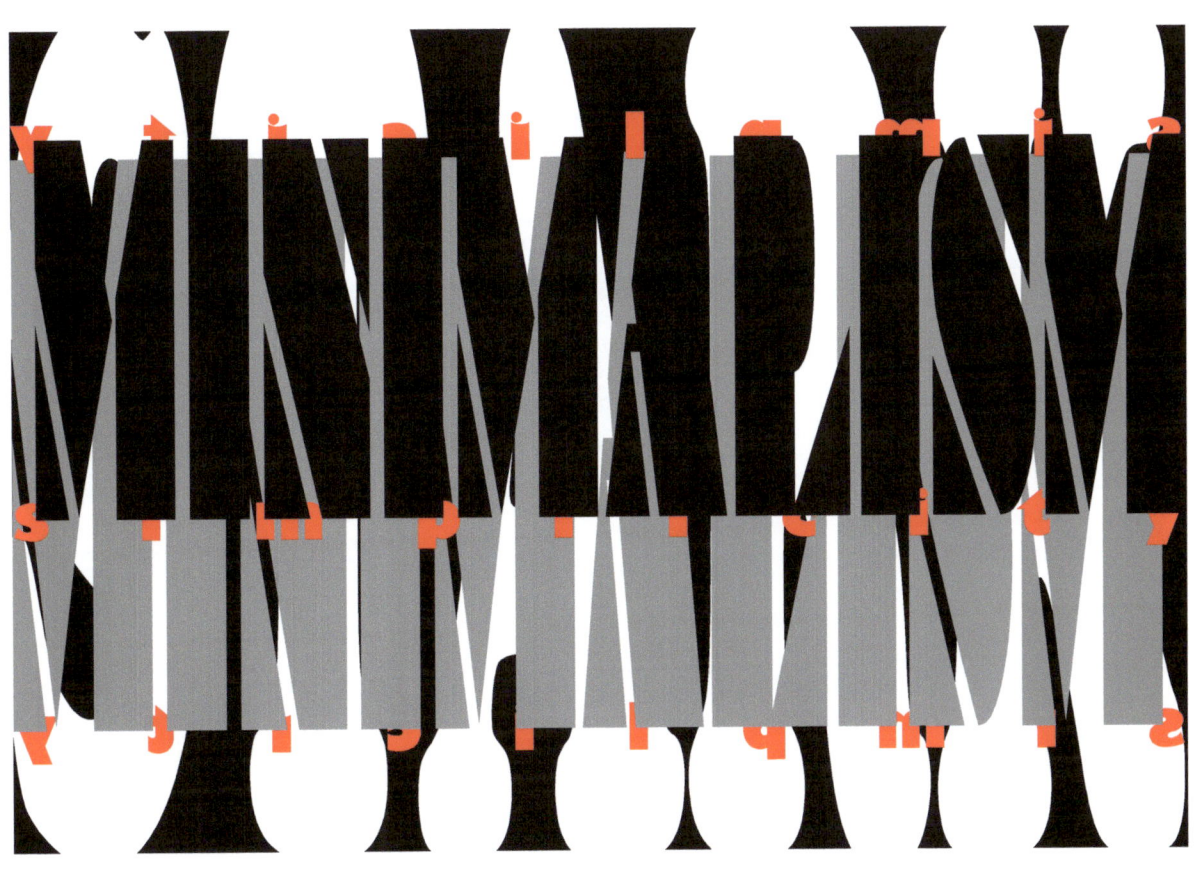

Keywords:

holy, trinity, love, faith, forgiveness

Keywords:

love, passion, adore, heart, blood, breath, comfortable, silence

They are all done by eric sprinkle.

ezesprinkle@gmail.com

ericsprinkle.com

ericsprinklearts.com

amazon.com/author/ericsprinkle